My Funeral, My Way

A Journal for Those Who Would Like to
Assist in Planning Their Own Funeral

Angela Hope De Simone

STORY MERCHANT BOOKS
BEVERLY HILLS
2014

THE STORY MERCHANT

My Funeral, My Way

Copyright © 2014 by Angela Hope De Simone

All rights reserved.

No part of this book may be reproduced or transmitted in any form or by any means, electronic or mechanical, including photocopying, recording, or by any information storage and retrieval system, without the express written permission of the author.

http://angelahopedesimone.wix.com/myfuneraljournal

Facebook: My Funeral, My Way
YouTube: My Funeral, My Way
Meet the Author, Angela Hope De Simone

Story Merchant Books
9601 Wilshire Boulevard #1202
Beverly Hills CA 90210

http://www.storymerchant.com/books.html

Editor: Lisa Cerasoli
Interior Design: Lisa Cerasoli & Danielle Canfield
Cover Photo: Karin De Finis
Cover Design: Leslie Taylor- BuffaloCreativeGroup.com

REVIEWS
My Funeral, My Way

"I found *My Funeral, My Way* to be a wonderful resource for families dealing with loss. How many times have I heard, "What would Mom have wanted?" or "What would Dad have wanted?" By keeping this journal, family members won't have to answer those questions, the questions are answered for them."

-Carl Goldstein

Goldsteins' Rosenberg
Raphael-Sacks Inc.
Funeral Home
Southampton, PA

"This book is a useful tool for aging individuals as well as entire families. As a nurse, I am often witness to uncertain medical outcomes among my patients. This book allows some sense of control at a time when many feel helpless. It is an excellent resource for patients and a concept long overdue. I would recommend this book without hesitation."

-Kathleen Bickings, RN

"*My Funeral, My Way* is an amazing, easy-to-follow guide for people approaching later life or end of life, to record their general wishes succeeding death. It is extremely user friendly, and is written with a warm, welcoming tone which creates comfort. This could serve as a great initial conversation piece among mourning family members."

-Amy Keiper-Shaw LCSW,QCSW, GC-C

Manager of Family Services
Chandler Hall Health Services
99 Barclay St. Newtown, PA

Dedication

I am most grateful to dedicate this book to my parents, Patricia and Anthony "Tug" DeFinis, who did their best to raise thirteen children in a three-bedroom row home in Philadelphia, Pennsylvania. They taught us to never be afraid of failing, to keep laughing, and to have faith.

To my husband, Chicky, of twenty-three years for his endless encouragement and great sense of humor.

To my children, Alyssa, 21, and Domenic, 14, who have made my life complete in every way.

I am certainly blessed to have you all!

Special Thanks...

To Janet and Dominick De Simone Sr. for their unconditional love and dedication to our family.

To my very, true friends who also happen to be my sisters! I appreciate all that you have done in co-parenting me and supporting me.

To my sisters, my best friends forever, Kathy and Eileen. I am immeasurably grateful to you for always encouraging me and keeping me laughing.

To my sisters, brothers, and all of our extended family members—aunts, uncles, nieces, nephews, and cousins: thank you!

To Lisa Cerasoli for your amazing way with words, and your patience, and guidance throughout this entire publishing process!

To Dr. Ken Atchity: thank you for believing in this book, and for all your expert, invaluable input. I'm honored to be a part of the Story Merchant library.

And to Christine Palumbo De Simone, PhD: thank you for your much needed expertise!

I love you all!

Introduction

Whose funeral is it, anyway? Why, it's yours, of course! Death is one topic that many people feel dreadfully uncomfortable discussing, especially when it's their own! Planning a funeral, burial, or service for a loved one can be devastating. So, why would you consider planning such a morbid event in advance? Well, it's because you may have the slightest desire to be included in at least a few of the decisions when planning your own funeral, burial or services. We are all among the living, and all living creatures must die sometime. I am sorry to be the one to break it to you, but it's true. As much as we hate to admit it, or refuse to think about it, it's the inevitable, and we will all have to leave this fantastic world as we know it.

Hopefully, you've had a predominantly healthy and fulfilling existence. Did you achieve your goals, follow your dreams, raise a family? Were you a good living person—a good friend, parent, parental figure, spouse, daughter or son? Were you a good role model? In your lifetime, did you travel, teach, volunteer, run a business, serve your community, become a caregiver, or become the person that you truly wanted to be? Everyone experiences good times and not-so-good times, but my wish for you is that you have done your best, and continue to do your best. Life sometimes takes us to places we never expected or wanted to be, yet here we are. It's never too late to make the best of the rest of our lives.

Now, with that said, when is the last time you attended a funeral, burial, or service for a deceased loved one or close friend? I am truly sorry for your loss. I offer my most sincere condolences to you, as well as the others who were affected by the death. Now think back. Did you find that the arrangements paid tribute to the deceased person? If the deceased person had been a close family member or friend, you already knew about their character, their loves, accomplishments, and family. On the other hand, perhaps the funeral was for an acquaintance or a perfect stranger. We often attend these services out of respect or obligation. And it's quite thoughtful and kind that you rearranged your schedule to attend. You may have had to cancel an important appointment or meeting, use a vacation day at work, or miss school to attend the services. I'm sure that your presence was much appreciated!

When I've been to services in the past, I know that I'm there to celebrate the life and mourn the death of the deceased, but sometimes I'd leave wishing that I had learned more about the person whom I had taken the time to honor. I wished that I would've left with a more intimate, personal connection to the deceased than when I arrived.

I believe that the attendees at a funeral, burial, or service deserve to learn more about the life and character of the deceased. Wouldn't you want everyone who attended *your* funeral, burial, or services to know what an amazing person you were? Wouldn't you like them to walk away with more than just tears and sadness? How about if they learned more about your hobbies and interests? What if they discovered that you rescued animals, loved children, took part in a particular sport, or enjoyed books, traveling, and classical music? Maybe they could have learned that you had contributed much of your time and energy to various charities. What about the awards you received, the offices you held, the organizations in which you were affiliated? Maybe the attendees would have liked to hear about your stage performances, favorite vacation destination, or favorite sports team.

I believe that if your service was personalized, family and guests who were in attendance might have a more intimate experience and leave with an everlasting impression of you and your life.

It has become more common these days for funeral services—especially for the elderly population—to be generic. Often, their funeral or burial arrangements seem to be planned and executed incorporating only the absolute bare necessities. This generic style seems to be rather cold and routine. We are all individuals, and I believe that each of us deserves an individualized and personalized final farewell. I'm sure that your loved ones, or whoever will be planning your funeral, will do their best to make your arrangements beautiful; but due to grief, and the time frame in which they have to work, it can be difficult to create the special and specific life celebration that you deserve. I'm not insinuating that this event should be viewed or thought of as enjoyable. I'm simply suggesting that each funeral or service can be an informative collection of memories from the life of the person we're honoring.

Why not refer to your services as your *Life Celebration* and be involved in its planning? This is the life that you have lived—with joy and sadness and triumph and love. You've worked hard all your life to create yourself. Why not say goodbye in a fashion all your own?

This is a *Funeral Journal*. It is a collection of personal thoughts and wishes that you'd like to be greatly considered to be incorporated into your own funeral/burial services. This is not a will; therefore, it is not binding in the court of law. Several topics covered in this journal may have likely been covered in your legal will. The *Funeral Journal* is not to be used as a disposition of assets. Rather, this journal is to be utilized solely as a preference guide for your loved ones to refer to at your passing.

The *Funeral Journal* serves two main purposes:

It's a template to make the necessary funeral arrangements easier for your family and loved ones. Having this reference guide can also alleviate disagreements, which often happen during times of stress and loss.

It's a security blanket. It lessens the burden for your family and loved ones in a time when they are grief-stricken and on a time constraint.

If you are unable to complete the Funeral Journal entirely, be assured that any information that you provide will be helpful and a useful tool in their planning process. Your family and loved ones will be better able to understand the decisions you have made and why you have made them. Please keep in mind that all of the requests in your journal may not be carried out perfectly; however, if this completed *Funeral Journal* is available, your requests can be considered. And what a great guide it will be. It's a gift to assist them in their efforts. Can you hear their sigh of relief? I can....

It is recommended that you read through the entire list of questions, options, and requests before completing your answers. Take your time. Jot down short answers, your thoughts on the subjects, until you have made a final decision. Make informed decisions. You may wish to discuss this with family, friends, funeral directors, or other professionals that you trust. I'm sure that your family or loved ones will be honored to help you complete your funeral journal. Most likely, they will appreciate your willingness to supply them with this information. They will respect you for taking this matter seriously, instead of pretending it will never happen. Do not allow anyone to convince you to make any of these decisions.

Although the topics discussed in this journal are not included in your everyday conversations, this may be a good time to open up to family and close friends as to the decisions you are contemplating.

The *Funeral Journal* will assist in generating conversations that may otherwise never be discussed. This may be a perfect time for all adult family members to complete their own *Funeral Journal*. If you are an adult, it's never too early to complete your own journal. You have the final say in completing your journal, and may decide not to share your journal or thoughts at this time. That is fine, too! This is your journal and these are your decisions!

Hopefully, you will do your best to personalize your *Life Celebration*. Most funeral professionals encourage the public to pre-arrange their services. This would be an ideal time to begin looking into the necessary products and services that are currently available. In contacting professional organizations with your questions, you have the opportunity to explore your options and become a better-informed consumer. There are many important details that you may want to include in the planning process. Your options are endless. You may decide that you have very few requests as far as your arrangements go. If that's the case, then you won't have much to fill in your journal. In the event that you discover some new options, you may be pleasantly surprised to discover that this journal will become an invaluable place where you can jot those wishes down.

Death is one topic that is difficult for many folks to discuss. Some feel that it is an extremely morbid subject, and they refuse to think or speak of it at all. Other folks may feel if they do not discuss this matter then it doesn't exist and won't happen. Unfortunately, it does exist in every family. Regardless of age, religion, race, health status, financial status, popularity, or title—death happens. You may choose denial. If you are in denial, revisit and complete this *Funeral Journal* when you're ready and willing to accept that all living beings will pass eventually.

Like the rest of you, I'm in no hurry to die. I'm looking forward to so much more life. Hopefully, I will live many more, healthy years—raising my children, watching them grow, and just enjoying them—while growing old with my husband, and continuing to spend time with the rest of our family and friends. However, in the meantime, when it is time for my demise, I definitely want to be included in the decisions concerning my final exit. Is that too much to ask? I don't think so!

Deciding when to begin? Well, why not now? Why wait until you reach a particular age or are diagnosed with a fatal illness? Don't wait until you are being wheeled into an unexpected surgery! This information in your completed *Funeral Journal* could be as important to you as a Living Will or Last Will in Testament. Would it be more sensible to make these personal decisions when you're feeling fairly well, and are alert, as opposed to being rushed or sick? Yes. So, begin when you're ready to face the simple fact that eventually we are all going to leave this earth, and you'd like to be included in your *Life Celebration*!

Inspiration

I was largely inspired to write this journal while in a funeral procession line of cars. The funeral was for a dear friend, Anthony. Anthony was my brother-in-law's father. Anthony was seventy years young, and was recently remarried. He had two adult sons and two grandchildren. He also had five sisters and a brother. Anthony was a tall, grey-haired Italian man from Philadelphia, Pennsylvania. He was a hard worker throughout his life and was a devoted father. I knew that he was a phenomenal brother upon whom all of his siblings relied for guidance and support. In fact, Anthony never turned away anyone in need. He loved to travel all over the country with his wife and his dog. Wherever Anthony went, he would take his dog along with him. He loved his dog, Scruffy, and enjoyed walking him in the park and playing with him. Anthony also loved to cook (Italian, of course). Anthony's homemade meatballs and ricotta cheese pies were a staple at every family function. He spent much of his time with his family, and, like many retired seniors, Anthony also spent a good bit of his time reconnecting with his religion. He attended weekly services at his church and was a member of Bible study groups there. He thoroughly enjoyed his retirement.

When Anthony became ill, he was informed by his physician that the end for him was near. From that point, Anthony lived for about five weeks. We all miss Anthony; his sons miss him terribly. He touched the hearts of numerous loves. I hope he knew how much he was loved!

Anthony was laid to rest in a somewhat traditional fashion. There was no mass or church arrangements. Christian services were held at a funeral home with an open casket, and then the funeral party continued to the cemetery for the burial. At the funeral parlor, friends, family, acquaintances, and church members—along with some other folks who didn't know Anthony at all—lined up to pay their respects. It was truly touching that each and every one of those people made it a priority to be there for Anthony's family at their time of loss. They actually had to take off work or school, find sitters, find transportation, or cancel appointments to attend these services. Anthony's family, although still grieving, was extremely friendly and welcoming to their guests. They were also quite appreciative to all who came to pay their respects.

At the front of the funeral parlor, the casket was placed open for everyone to view. Many guests kneeled at the side of the casket as they viewed his body and prayed silently. Anthony's two sons stood alongside of their father's casket greeting their guests with handshakes and hugs. When the last of the guests had paid their respects, the pastor led the crowd in prayer. He quoted verse after verse from the Bible, while proceeding to divulge the precise page number where each verse could be found. Then, the pastor spoke of his recent conversations with Anthony. They were interesting and informative. The pastor concluded his tribute with how much Anthony loved his family. I was glad and felt so lucky that I had known Anthony when he was alive.

After leaving the funeral parlor, I sat in the car with my husband waiting for the vehicle procession to begin moving toward the cemetery. At that moment, I realized that Anthony's arrangements did not give any inclination about the person that he was in his life. Given the time frame to plan, I'm sure his grief-stricken family did their best. His family adored him and he knew it in life, which is very important. But many folks came to celebrate with us who didn't know him like I did. And I wished that the service would have represented Anthony for the unique dog-loving, Italian-cooking, warm, loving world traveler that he was.

This would not be the first time that I left a funeral wanting to learn more about the life of the deceased. I know that sounds very bizarre. Of course, it was heartbreaking and I felt so terrible for the grief that his family was encountering. I guess I felt that Anthony deserved much more, and so did the funeral attendees. I wondered if all of those fine people who came to pay their respects to Anthony's family wanted to know more about him. Maybe I just wanted them to learn more. I felt that this service did not do justice to such a good living man, with good morals, funny stories, and astounding accomplishments. I wanted everyone to know more about the man whose funeral they were attending.

That was the exact moment that I realized that I wanted to be the coordinator for my own funeral. I decided that I needed to be included in the planning process. I also want others to be aware that they can make any, or all, of their planning decisions just as easily. Just complete the information in your *Funeral Journal* and *voilà*, your mission is accomplished. Then, when you're ready, tell a family member or loved one that your completed book exists, and where it may be found—for when it is needed.

Another inspirational funeral that I have attended was for my aunt Mary. She was the mother of six adult children and a grandmother of eighteen. Like Anthony, she was a wonderful person. She was sixty-five years old, and, also like Anthony, was ill before she passed.

When we entered the funeral home for her viewing, the podium in the foyer held a "sign-in" registry. As we approached the viewing area, on a small wooden table sat an open book that read, *Please tell us something funny or inspiring that you remember about our mother*. I could not wait to write a funny story (short, of course) that I remembered about her. I also wanted to glance through the other responses that were written before mine. Beside the table, closer to the viewing area, prominently stood three wooden easels that had been decorated with collages of family photos. This was certainly a great way for everyone to learn a little more about the person, sister, mother, friend, daughter, nurse, aunt, and grandmother that Mary was. She was laid to rest in a beautiful red dress that she wore for one of her children's weddings.

Mary was a Catholic, so a high mass was held in her honor. About ten minutes into the mass, her son Tom approached the altar and began to speak. "For those of you who did not know my mother very well, I would like to take a few minutes to tell you a little about her life..." He spoke about how Mary was one of ten children. She had raised six children on her own. He spoke about how she had gone back to nursing school and worked in the maternity ward in a local hospital for nearly thirty years. He spoke about her being a devoted grandmother of eighteen grandchildren and how she still insisted on caring for them while she was sick and needed care herself.

Tom did not read any of this. His words came straight from his heart. It was an unbelievable tribute to his mother. Lastly, Tom created music, CDs that included ten of his mother's favorite songs. Those CDs were given out to the immediate family and her sisters. I will never forget how touched I felt when I went home.

By no means am I attempting to compare these two funeral services. I am simply suggesting that if given the opportunity, the deceased may have had a few suggestions regarding their services.

Whenever I discuss these topics with friends or family, I find that most folks have many opinions about funerals, services, and burials—other than the obvious reason for being there. Some feel strongly about certain options regarding their arrangements. This is your opportunity to make your wishes known. Perhaps you feel that you definitely do not want to be cremated, or you prefer not to be buried. No one will know how you feel about these issues unless you make it known. This journal is a great way to inform others of your wishes. If you're not sure about a particular issue, just skip that option in your journal, then go back to it later, after you research it a little further. If you decide that a particular subject does not affect you at all, just cross it out and move on to the next one. Another benefit of this journal is that you have the freedom to change the information about your decisions at any time. It belongs to you, so you have complete control over who reads it, too. As long as you write legibly, you will be just fine. No one will be grading your *Funeral Journal* for spelling errors or neatness. I cannot emphasize enough about taking your time, making informed decisions, and being creative! After all, whose funeral is it anyway?

My sister Frances, who is forty-eight years old, has decided that she does not wish to have a traditional funeral or burial. Although she was raised Catholic, her decisions for her *Life Celebration* are somewhat untraditional. She wishes to be cremated when she passes. She has not decided at this time what she would want done with her ashes after cremation. She does, however, have a strong interest in having a party-like celebration in place of a traditional church ceremony. In her opinion, she feels that a mass in Church would be too depressing. She would like for family, friends, and attendees to enjoy music, dancing, and cocktails. The guests will be encouraged to speak about their memories of Frances and reminisce about good times spent together. This will be her way to celebrate her life while allowing guests to mourn. Frances does not want to have any type of viewing or wake. She feels that a party-like celebration would be the perfect way for her family and close friends to have the closure they require. This is her personal preference. Why should it be planned differently?

When speaking with one of my clients, Joanne, about her feelings regarding her own funeral or services, she willingly expressed her one and only request: She is an extremely casual person, and when she is laid to rest, she would like to be wearing a fashionable warm-up suit. This is Joanne's way of conveying the type of person she was to all attending her service. She is a casual, loving and non-pretentious person. Joanne is Jewish, but this clothing selection is not typical in the Jewish funeral tradition, and neither is an open casket. Joanne's request will never be granted—or at least discussed amongst her surviving family members—if she does not have it conveyed in her *Funeral Journal*.

Upon discussing this topic with my friend, Jeff, without hesitation, he expressed that he wanted to be cremated. After cremation, he wishes for his ashes to be distributed in the baseball field where he spent so much time playing ball with his friends. Those were the best years of his life, and this request was very important to him. Unless he discussed this topic with his wife and family—which he hadn't—how would they know what his wishes were? Why shouldn't his wishes be granted? Who should make these decisions for him? Why should someone else make assumptions about what he would want? Expressing his feelings and requests in his *Funeral Journal* avoids the guesswork.

So, let us begin!

This Journal Belongs To:

_____

My Funeral Journal

Today's date?

_____

What is your full name?

_____

What is your date of birth?

_____

Where is your place of birth? (City, State, Country)

_____

_____

_____

Who are your birth parents?

_____

_____

Are you adopted?

_____

Are you married? If so, what is your partner's name?

_____

_____

Do you have any children? If so, please list their names and ages.

_____

_____

_____

Do you currently have any pets? If so, please list their names and types.

_____

_____

_____

_____

Who would you like to care for your pets at the time of your passing?

_____

_____

_____

_____

Keep in mind that while in your Will you may name this person, many Wills are not read until months after the funeral. If you choose at this time to designate someone to be responsible for your pets, your pets will be cared for

My Funeral, My Way

by them immediately. Also, it will be easier on those focusing on taking care of your final wishes.

*It is best to discuss this decision with the person you choose ahead of time, to make sure they are willing to take on this responsibility.

Do you practice a religion? If so, what is it? Are you religious?

_____

_____

_____

Should your religion be considered when making the following funeral/services/burial arrangements?

_____

_____

Would you prefer a non-religious funeral?

_____

_____

Do you have a Last Will and Testament?

_____

Do you have a Living Will?

_____

Where can these important documents be found in the event of your death?

_____

_____

_____

Are you an organ donor? In order to be considered for organ donation, you must register within your state as, "Organ Donor." This question is usually asked by the Department of Motor Vehicles when you renew your driver's license or obtain a new driver's license. For more information about organ donation, visit the website: www.organdonor.gov.

_____

Who would you like to handle the following arrangements in the event of your death?

Name

_____

_____

_____

Relationship

_____
_____
_____

Phone Number

_____

Why have you chosen this person?

_____
_____
_____
_____

Do you currently have a Life Insurance policy? If so, where can this important document be found? This document is helpful when making final funeral arrangements, as life insurance benefits may affect your loved ones' out-of-pocket expenses.

_____
_____
_____
_____

Other than your insurance policy, do you have funds saved for these funeral expenses? If so, please give details, or tell someone that you trust with this information.

_____

_____

_____

_____

In addition to your family members and friends, is there anyone else that you would like notified in the event of your passing? Please indicate their names and telephone or cell phone numbers.

Name   Phone Number

_____

_____

_____

_____

_____

_____

_____

My Funeral, My Way

Is there anyone that you strongly feel should not be informed of your death?

_____
_____
_____
_____

Give the reason, if you wish.

_____
_____
_____
_____

Is there anyone that you do not wish to attend your funeral? If so, and you would like to give the reason, you may do so below.

_____
_____
_____
_____
_____
_____

Death Notice/Obituary

Would you like your death notice/obituary to appear in your local newspaper? If so, what is the name of the publication?

_____

_____

_____

_____

The funeral home will usually take care of publishing your funeral announcement, which typically includes the following information:

- Full name and maiden name if applicable
- Immediate relatives/ family
- City, state, and town where you recently lived
- Donations sites to be made in lieu of flowers in your memory

In addition to your local newspaper, is there another newspaper or publication in which you would like your death notice/obituary to be advertised? Example: A local newspaper in a neighborhood where you grew up or lived in for an extended period of time.

_____

_____

_____

_____

You may create your own death announcement/obituary to be published. If you do choose this option, you will be assured that what the public reads is exactly what you want them to know and remember. There are numerous topics that you may wish to include in your announcement, as well as the typical information that the funeral home provides (see above}.

This is a list of some of the options that you may wish to consider in your personal obituary.

*Nickname
*City and state where you were born
*City and state where you most recently lived
*Your education

My Funeral, My Way

*Your occupations

*Your military service information (dates and locations you have served)

*Your marriage information (date and location of wedding)

 *Your children and grandchildren's names

*Your hobbies, interests, memberships, offices held, sports played

*Your favorite sports teams, favorite family vacation destinations

Include what you would like to be remembered for most!

Be creative when writing your own obituary! It was your life, and you have the power to convey the highlights of your amazing journey!

Angela Hope De Simone

MY OBITUARY

_____

_____

_____

_____

_____

_____

_____

_____

_____

_____

_____

_____

_____

_____

_____

My Funeral, My Way

_____

_____

_____

_____

_____

Is there anything that you would not like to be included in your death notice?

_____

_____

_____

_____

Would you like a photograph of yourself to be posted with your death notice/obituary? Do you have a particular photo in mind? If so, label the back of the photo and attach it to this page.

_____

_____

_____

Costs and Considerations

When making some of the decisions in planning your own services, funeral, cremation, or burial, be sure to consider the costs for these expenses. You will not need to make these decisions today, but when you are considering the endless options, be realistic! A solid gold casket or a funeral mass held at the Vatican in Rome may not be feasible for your family or budget. (Or maybe it is!)

Usually, the funeral director will include the cost of the death notice in their professional fees. They will place the death notice—sometimes including a photograph of the deceased—in the local newspaper with the family's assistance. This is how the family and guests receive the funeral, burial, or services information along with locations and times.

Scattering cremation remains can be provided by funeral professionals. The costs depend on the destination. Families often choose to scatter ashes on their own.

Angela Hope De Simone

There is an extensive variety of products and services offered by professionals that you may or may not wish to use. We wanted to give you a general idea of several of the most popular options. *But who says that you have to go with the most popular options?* You should follow your own heart and mind before making these decisions.

For accurate prices, contact your local professional funeral service providers. Funeral directors will be more than pleased to furnish you with costs for their products and services, and they are always willing to answer your questions. Many funeral homes will offer and encourage you to pre-arrange and pre-pay for your services, but do not allow anyone to pressure you into making hasty decisions. You may want to create a list of your questions and concerns before you contact the professionals. Provided below are some topics on which to base your questions. The initial call that you make to a funeral professional should be either to request a brochure of their products and services, or to ask them the questions from your list. This way, you will be making informed decisions. It is a good idea to get a few estimates, and to review all of your options before making any final decisions or pre-payments. Most of the services and products for this type of event may be pre-arranged, and then paid for at the time of service. With that said, when you contact a trusted funeral professional, they will be exceptionally helpful in answering questions, and will assist you in planning your *Life Celebration*.

Use this list to guide your questions when contacting a funeral professional:

1. Traditional burial
2. Cremation
3. Cemetery plot
4. Graveside services
5. Grave marker/tombstone
6. Mausoleum
7. Scattering of ashes
8. Funeral/religious services provided
9. Funeral announcements/obituary
10. Eulogy allotments

11. Music allotments

12. Prices/Payments for products and services

Take your time, get informed, be creative, and talk about your thoughts with others, if you wish.

Funeral Home Services

Every funeral is different. Your options are only limited by the boundaries of your imagination.

There are numerous factors to consider when planning an event such as a funeral. Most of these details are based on preference, costs, religious beliefs, and the actual funeral coordinator.

Will you or someone else be responsible for the costs involved in your funeral, burial or cremation services?

_____

_____

_____

Would you like to have your services performed in a funeral home?

_____

_____

_____

Do you know which funeral home you would like to use, or would you prefer your family members make that decision? If you do know which funeral home you'd prefer, please give the full name and address below.

_____
_____
_____
_____

Have you or your family members used this funeral home in the past?

_____
_____
_____
_____

Why have you chosen this funeral home?

_____
_____
_____
_____

My Funeral, My Way

At this point, have you made funeral, burial, or cremation arrangements for yourself? If yes, please explain what type of arrangements you have made and with whom. Include the amount of deposits or fees that you have paid thus far, and to whom these fees were paid.

_____

_____

_____

_____

_____

_____

Do you have a receipt for these deposits or fees? If so, please attach it to this page.

What is the name of the contact person with whom you have made arrangements?

Name:

_____

Email:

_____

Address:

_____

_____

_____

_____

Phone Number:

_____

*Be sure to get the contact person's full name and always get a receipt for fees/deposits made.

Graveside Services

These services are performed when the burial vault is delivered to the cemetery on the day of the actual services. The clergy or officiant will then hold the services at the cemetery along the graveside with family and guests present. When services are concluded, the family and guests may simply depart.

Is this option a tradition in your family? Would you like graveside services held in lieu of traditional services in a church? If so, why have you made this decision?

_____
_____
_____
_____
_____
_____
_____
_____

Visitation

During a viewing or wake, the casket can be kept open for all guests to view, or it can be kept closed completely. When possible, most families will choose to keep their loved one's casket open. In some cultures, an open casket is not an option because of their religious beliefs or traditions. This is an opportunity for mourners to pay their respects and offer their sympathy to one another.

If possible, would you like your body to be viewed in an open casket?

_____

_____

Why have you made this decision?

_____

_____

_____

_____

Clothing

What type of clothing would you like to be wearing when you are buried? In some religions, a particular type of clothing is traditional. You may choose clothing that best represents you and the life you have lived. This outfit may be in your possession at this time (example: military uniform, wedding dress, bowling league attire, sports jersey, police uniform, etc.) It is your choice, so be creative.

What type of clothing would you like to be wearing when you are buried? Why have you chosen this outfit?

_____
_____
_____
_____
_____
_____

Do you currently own this outfit or will it need to be purchased prior to the funeral?

_____

_____

Do you currently wear glasses?

_____

_____

If so, do you want to be wearing your glasses when you are buried?

_____

_____

Jewelry

Do you have a special piece of jewelry that you would like to be wearing when you are buried? It may be an item that holds a special meaning to you (example: wedding ring, earrings, class ring, favorite pendant, etc.).

Before making this important decision, you may want to consider the idea of passing one of these items onto a close family member. The item will become an heirloom and will be cherished forever.

What jewelry would you like to wear when you are laid to rest? What special meaning does it have to you?

_____
_____
_____
_____
_____
_____

Additional Personal Items

Do you have a particular item or items that are truly special to you? Is this item something that you would like buried with you? (Example: rosary, golf club, an award, military badge of honor, photos, etc.)

Which items would you like to be buried with and why?

_____
_____
_____
_____
_____
_____

Public Display of Personal Items

At many funeral services, important personal items that belong to the deceased are displayed for all to view. Personal items displayed are a simple way to feel closer on a more personal level to the deceased. I believe this option to be an extremely important method to allow the guests to learn more about your life in the way that you would like to be remembered. (Examples: a stethoscope, fire helmet, sports jersey, awards, trophies, bowling ball, art work, musical instrument, photos of your favorite pets, vacation photos, family photos or any other items that would best describe you!)

Which personal items would you like to be temporarily displayed at your services? These items will not be buried with you.

_____

_____

_____

_____

_____

_____

_____

_____

Memory Cards

At most funeral services, memory cards are available for guests to keep in remembrance of the deceased. They typically have a picture on one side, which is usually a religious figure, a peaceful scene, or a photo of the deceased themselves. The reverse side states the name, the dates of the deceased's birth and death, and typically a prayer, poem, or a selected verse. These are usually provided by the funeral director and are custom-made according to the family's requests.

Do you have suggestions for a picture or a particular poem, favorite verse, or prayer that you would like to be used?

_____
_____
_____
_____
_____

Pall Bearers

Whenever a casket is used, Pall Bearers are required to assist the funeral directors with transporting and maneuvering the casket during and between services. There are usually six to eight Pall Bearers used for the service.

Who would you prefer to be your Pall Bearers? If you have no preference, simply state "NO PREFERENCE."

_____

_____

_____

_____

_____

_____

*If a family is in need of Pall Bearers, most funeral homes will provide this service (using their employees) for an additional fee.

Cremation

If you choose to be cremated, please explain why you have made this decision. This will help your loved ones better understand your wish.

_____

_____

_____

_____

What would you like to be done with your ashes after cremation? Why have you made this decision?

_____

_____

_____

_____

There are numerous options for how your ashes could be contained, and many places where your ashes could be scattered. You may use your own creativity. Some folks have their ashes scattered in one particular place like a beach, ocean, or ball field. It may be one of your favorite places to visit or vacation. Other folks wish their ashes to be kept in urns in a loved one's home or placed in parts of the jewelry of their loved ones. Another option you may consider is to divide your ashes. This allows them to be placed in an urn, in jewelry, and at a particular destination. Again, your options are endless.

*There are private companies that will perform the scattering of ashes for those families who are unable to carry out the scattering themselves. There are also private companies that will perform "burials at sea" for cremations. Hopefully, your family will not have any problems carrying out your final wishes.

Burial

Do you want a traditional burial in a cemetery?

_____

_____

_____

_____

Do you have a cemetery plot arranged?

_____

_____

_____

What is the full name and address of the cemetery that you would like to use for your burial?

_____

_____

_____

_____

Why have you chosen this cemetery?

_____

_____

_____

_____

Do you have family members buried in this cemetery? If so, you may list their names below.

_____

_____

_____

_____

_____

Do you want a private burial? If so, why have you made this decision?

_____

_____

_____

_____

_____

My Funeral, My Way

Would you prefer a mausoleum for your burial? If so, where?

_____
_____
_____

Have you made prior arrangements for a mausoleum burial? If so, why have you chosen this option?

_____
_____
_____

*Few cemeteries continue to offer the option of a mausoleum, but you may have access to one from prior arrangements.

Tombstone/Grave Marker

What type of grave marker would you like to be displayed at your grave?

Color:
_____

Shape:
_____

Design:
_____
_____
_____

Size:
_____

Comments to be engraved:
_____
_____
_____
_____

My Funeral, My Way

Would you like your photo to be placed on your grave marker?

_____

_____

If so, please label the photo and attach it to this page.

*Keep in mind that several cemeteries no longer allow grave markers that stand more than a few inches above the ground. This policy change is due to landscaping and the general upkeep of the cemetery grounds. Be sure to check with your cemetery for their policy on grave markers before making your final decision.

Services

Would you like funeral services to be held for you?

_____

_____

Where would you like for these services to take place? (Examples: a place of worship, funeral home, cemetery, or you may choose any place you would like.)

If you would like your funeral services to be held in a place of worship, where would this be? Please give the full name and address of this location and the reason why you have chosen it.

_____

_____

_____

_____

_____

_____

Do you have a particular celebrant that you would like to conduct your services if possible? (Examples: rabbi, priest, pastor, minister, or other religious leader.)

_____
_____
_____
_____
_____

Is there a particular psalm or prayer that you would like to be read at your services? If so, what is it?

_____
_____
_____
_____
_____
_____
_____
_____

Eulogy

When a guest, family member, or clergy member speaks on your behalf at your services, about you and the life you have lived, they are giving your eulogy.

Would you prefer a close family member or friend to give your eulogy at your services? If so, who have you chosen, and why have you chosen this person?

_____

_____

_____

_____

You may choose to write your own eulogy or special thoughts to be read at your services. I believe this to be the most interesting aspect of any funeral service. You have the opportunity to tell your own story and convey to others a collection of your own personal views from life. If you do want your own words and thoughts read aloud, write them in the space provided below. This may be the last time your own thoughts will be spoken in public. This writing piece can be short, simple and light-hearted. You may choose to write your eulogy in a deeper and more serious fashion, which might make it lengthy, too. It could be very interesting if you added a bit of humor, too, but it's your choice. You will not be graded on your neatness, spelling, or sentence structure. I'm sure you will do a fine job, and your eulogy will be read aloud and enjoyed by all!

Some options to consider when writing your Eulogy are:

*Your best qualities

*Your favorite sports, sports teams, music or musicians

*Personality traits that you are proud to have

*Your most cherished friendships

*Your love for your family

*Your love for your favorite pets

*What/who is closest to your heart?

*How you would like others to remember you?

My Funeral, My Way

MY EULOGY

Angela Hope De Simone

Readings

Do you have a favorite poem (religious or non-religious) that you'd like to have read at your services? If so, please keep a labeled copy in this journal for easy reference. You can choose a few of your favorites. It's your funeral service, and your decision to make.

Please list the title and author of the poem(s) or verse(s) that you wish to use. If possible, place a labeled copy of this material in your journal to have for easy access.

Title_____

Author_____

Title_____

Author_____

Title_____

Author_____

Title_____

Author_____

Title_____

Author_____

Who would you prefer to do the readings at your service?

_____

_____

_____

_____

Music

Many houses of worship have their own organist/vocalist that will perform for these services. Would you like an organist/vocalist to perform at your services?

_____

_____

Would you like a musician or choir to perform at your services? If you would like to use an outside performer, I'm sure that could easily be arranged. (Examples: bagpipes, harpist, organist, guitarist, flutist, pianist, etc.)

_____

_____

If you want an outside performer, who would you like? If you do not know of one, you may allow that decision to be made for you.

_____

_____

_____

Do you have a favorite song or hymn that you would like to be sung or played at your services? What is the title? Where can it be found?

_____
_____
_____
_____

Would you like pre-recorded music to be played at any of your services? List those songs/artists below and specify where you would like this music to be played. (Example: in church, or at the funeral services.)

_____
_____
_____

Song_____
Artist_____

Song_____
Artist_____

Veteran

Are you a veteran?

_____

In which branch of the military did you serve? What was your title/rank?

_____

_____

Which years did you serve?

_____

Where did you serve?

_____

_____

Many veteran funeral services may include a veteran salute/tribute. This occurs when current service members make a brief appearance at the funeral service of a veteran. At that time, a trumpet will be played in honor of the deceased, and a flag will be presented to the family of the deceased veteran. From my experience, this tribute is an everlasting honor and is a magnificent way to recognize your service to your country.

So, with this said, would you consider having a veteran salute/ tribute at your funeral or services?

_____

_____

_____

_____

Name Tags

A recent tradition has been introduced that seems to be gaining popularity. While many family members are greeting guests, they are spending a good bit of time introducing themselves and others. This task becomes time consuming and often awkward and exhausting for both family and guests.

We are not expected to know everybody by name, especially at this type of event, but more and more families are requesting that their family and guests wear their name on a sticker. Name stickers are filled out by the guests and worn in the funeral home or anywhere that guests are greeted. This, of course, is optional for guests, but does allow for a friendlier atmosphere for all attending. How many times were you a guest at a funeral and had difficulty recognizing other guests or family members? It seems we leave those events a little confused, but greeting and thanking guests become less stressful when names are prominently displayed. This is evidently a sad and complicated event, so why not make it easier for all involved?

Would you like your guests to wear name tags at your funeral/burial services?

_____

_____

_____

Flowers

One of the first items to be ordered for most funeral/burial services is flowers. The amazing aroma and the beautiful arrangements that fill the atmosphere are immediately captured upon our first steps into a funeral service. The live floral tribute symbolizes life. Also, when a family member is lost, friends want to do something to help comfort their loved ones. Often, flower arrangements are ordered and sent to the immediate family. Flowers look lovely, smell delightful, and assist in decorating the funeral home, place of worship, and cemetery.

There is a wide variety of flowers and many colors from which to choose. There are also several different styles of arrangements traditionally used for this occasion. Some of the options for funeral flowers are casket sprays, crosses, wreaths, heart-shaped arrangements, bouquets, and rosaries.

Do you have a favorite flower? Do you have a favorite color of flower? I'm sure it would be helpful to your family and loved ones to know this information.

Which flower would you most like to have displayed at your services?

_____

_____

_____

Do you have one particular florist that you would like to use? If so, please list the business name, email, phone, and address below.

_____

_____

_____

_____

Why have you chosen this florist?

_____

_____

_____

Donation to Charity "in Lieu" of Flowers

This option has become quite popular. Family members will request that instead of sending flowers to the funeral home, church, or synagogue, donations can be sent to a particular charity or organization. You may personally select the charity or organization that you wish to receive the donations. When choosing your favorite charity, consider one in which you have a strong interest or involvement.

Would you like donations to be sent to your favorite charity or organization in lieu of flowers? If so, which charity or organization would you like donations to be sent? Why have you made this decision?

_____
_____
_____
_____
_____

Drive-by

It is tradition in various cultures that the funeral procession (line of vehicles) drives from the memorial site and passes by the home of the deceased on the way to the cemetery. Traditionally, it is to show respect to the life of the deceased.

Would you like the funeral procession to drive by your home on the way to the cemetery?

_____
_____
_____
_____
_____
_____

Additional Requests

Do you have any other requests to be included in the planning of your funeral, services, or burial that have not been previously discussed in this *Funeral Journal*? If so, please list and describe your ideas or requests on the lines below.

_____

_____

_____

_____

_____

_____

_____

_____

_____

_____

_____

_____

You Have Completed Your Funeral Journal....Now What?

Congratulations! You have completed your *Funeral Journal*. You took your time to do your best in planning the funeral you have imagined. Keep this journal in a safe place so that it is easy to find when it is needed. Now that it is completed, you have a few options to make certain your journal is read and your wishes are fulfilled.

You could give your journal to a loved one you trust so that they can refer to it when the time has come.

Alternatively, you could make a note in your Will informing your trustees where to locate your journal, and how to use it.

Either way, your *Funeral Journal* will be extremely useful in the planning process. Again, congratulations on being proactive in planning your *Life Celebration*.

Hopefully, you have loved deeply, and felt deeply loved throughout this amazing journey we call life. I hope there will be many more accomplishments and dreams that you will fulfill. And I hope this journal represents "peace" to you—peace of mind. You can fill it out, tuck it away, and then go live and let your memories multiply far into the future!

About the Author

Angela "Angel" Hope De Simone was born and raised in the far Northeast section of Philadelphia, Pennsylvania, into a family of fifteen. She's the youngest child in a baker's dozen—which includes five brothers and seven sisters, all of whom assisted in her upbringing.

Ms. De Simone attended Pierce Junior College, located in Philadelphia, where she received her associate's degree in business, and met her husband. After working in the business industry for over eight years, she decided to pursue her dream of helping others by becoming a licensed massage therapist. She has been practicing massage therapy for eighteen years.

She currently resides in Newtown, Pennsylvania, with her husband, Chicky, and two children, Alyssa and Domenic.

Angel is a journal junkie—been keeping one since she was seven. In her free time she loves antiquing, and arts & crafts. Her specialty is carving inspirational words and sayings into chairs, mirrors, etc. She has an ETSY page where you can see and purchase her original artwork!

Her favorite beach destination is "Cape May." And she is known in her circle of friends for her punctuality. Angel is a very spiritual person. She owns a sixteen-year-old cat, Belle, and Denise—a retired race dog, a greyhound, that she personally rescued. Angel is also a big fan of 80's tunes.

And, yes, you will find most of this trivia, that is unique to Angel, decorating the pages of her very own Funeral Journal.

This is Angel De Simone's first book.

Made in the USA
Charleston, SC
25 May 2014